Inside Outlandish

by Susan Tuttle
illustrations by ANNA

Bergli Books
Riehen, Switzerland

Inside Outlandish

Bergli Books Ltd.
Aeuss. Baselstrasse
CH-4125 Riehen
Switzerland

Tel.: +41 (0)61 601 31 01
Fax: +41 (0)61 601 67 01
E-mail:
berglibooks@compuserve.com

'Cawfee and Rösti' and 'Behind those closed curtains'
first appeared in *Ticking Along Too*, 1990 and 1996, Bergli
Books Ltd. Some of the stories in this collection originally
appeared in the English language quarterly *New Roots*,
1989-1997

ISBN 3-9520002-8-0

Believing in someone is the first part.
The second part is believing in one's self.
This book is for the people in my life
who patiently waited for me to get
the second part right.

Contents

Cawfee and *Rösti*

I was born in New Jersey to a Swiss father and a German mother. But my mother grew up in New 'Joyzee' which becomes evident when she is 'tawking', making 'cawfee', or going to see a movie at the 'thayater'. Nevertheless, she makes *Rösti, Fleischkäse* and *Bauernbrot* for my father when he's home on Saturdays watching baseball on TV.

I never gave much thought to my multi-national background. In the States lots of people can lay claim to a mix of cultures in their home life. I considered myself American. But I became curious about my Swiss roots, about this nationality I possessed complete with red passport and a *Heimatort* (home town) simply because my father was a Swiss. I moved to Switzerland.

Armed with a little high school German and a name with authentic ethnic origins, I quickly realized that I needed more to break into a culture which I had thought belonged somewhat to me. My American-ness, even though somewhat softened by the European base of my upbringing, suddenly became an issue worthy of every neighbor's attention. In Switzerland they regarded me as *Fremde*, a foreigner.

Things got a bit complicated when I, a Swiss who had grown up in America, fell in love with Andy, an American who had grown up in Switzerland. Everyone had always thought he was Swiss so when we got married they presumed I obtained my Swiss passport through him. At that time a foreign woman marrying a Swiss automatically became a Swiss – later, when the laws changed, Andy got his Swiss citizenship through *me*. Trying to clarify this was very confusing at times. Our friends laughed and called us the 'odd couple' – a Swiss who could hardly speak a Swiss language marrying an American who had always passed as a Swiss.

As the years go by, I find I can get by pretty well with the language. I can read the newspapers and carry on a conversation in Swiss-German. But sometimes there is a catch in the level of my understanding. It *seems* as if I am quite fluent at times. That will give the person who is speaking with me the confidence to rattle on, forgetful that my language skills might be lagging behind a bit. Then I have to concentrate hard to catch the surface meaning. I may not be able to grasp any deeper significance from intonation or word choice.

When someone has to stop to clarify the meaning, it can work to my advantage. I may only want to ask what a word means and check that I understood something correctly at a very basic grammatical level. But my questions are often misinterpreted as much deeper interest in whatever topic is at hand. People appreciate that. My hard

2

listening is interpreted as good listening. Then I have to listen even harder.

But being liked for being a good listener – to Frau Müller's latest illness and Frau Schmidt's problem with the *Waschküche* (laundry room) schedule – is not as rewarding as being liked for who you are. This is difficult because I just don't feel like myself when I speak German. I'm not aware of my accent in German but I know those listening to me are. How does it change their impression of me? I dread the idea of sounding 'cute' with my errors. I don't want to be tedious or make people have to work hard to understand me.

I can't be very humorous or spontaneous in German and I can't seem to include subtle nuances of meaning. I'm restricted to communication in a basic form, void of personal touches. I suspect that true fluency includes one's personality as well as one's linguistic skills. I do not feel I am that fluent yet. Is it possible to reach this level in a foreign language? The union of thought and word is comfortably and intimately rooted in my mind in English. Even if I could lay claim to fluency in another language, my true vehicle of expression would still be English. And American English at that. Living here with another language is like being put into linguistic exile.

Written expression is very important to me. I like to write and then let my readers have the pleasant surprise of identification as they suddenly realize that they've seen that, been there or felt the same once. The reader of what I write is an essential part of my writing. When I wrote in America, I depended on the audience sharing with me a common bank of knowledge, feelings and experiences from which I could draw my inspiration.

But for whom do I write in Switzerland? What do I share with my audience here that I can offer them back in prose? Writing as an American in Switzerland, I would always be the foreigner. Can I write as a Swiss for the Swiss in English? I am still the foreigner.

Is it language alone which perpetuates this feeling of foreign-ness? Or is there something else to it? How does one get 'in'? It seems as if language could be blamed for a lot of my troubles with expression, being understood and understanding. But perhaps the real root of the problem lies in having two cultures without calling either one home. Maybe I really am a Swiss who has simply been away too long. Sometimes I realize I am not letting Switzerland in for *cawfee* or for *Rösti*. The American voice inside me says, "Come on in, the door's open!" But my Swiss voice asks, "Do I know you?"

Du's and don'ts

I have to admit that I resented having to choose between *Sie* and *Du* when first initiated into the German language. I remember well my anguish when introduced to an elderly Swiss uncle. Since I had never met him before, he was a stranger, requiring the *Sie* form. But then he was family, entitled to a *Du*. So great was my confusion that I wound up alternating *Sie's* with *Du's*.

This situation made me so uncomfortable that I decided to use the formal form with everyone I spoke to in German. It did have a consequence: looking like a complete idiot in front of children. Their surprise at being called *Sie* was always followed by incredulous laughter.

As I finally accustomed myself to the absurdity of having two you's to choose from, I decided it was time to break the rules and set a new precedent. I would anglicize the entire language single-handedly and call everyone *Du*: equality for all. My attempts only went over well with the kids in my son's kindergarten, at the local trendy Swedish furniture store, and at the alternative health food store. Outside of that the reactions were cool at their warmest.

But I persisted. I made *Dutzis* with a rather proper, staid neighbor of mine. She was surprised because being my senior she was the one who should have initiated it. Plus our only contact was spotting one another at the mailbox from time to time.

We avoided greeting each other for about a month afterwards. Then, one day while retreating from the mailbox, I realized with a queer lightening of my heart that we had both resorted to the old familiarly formal *Sie*. We never were meant to be *Du*. And suddenly I understood something.

Soon after this episode we moved back to the States for a year. I thought with some satisfaction that now I could forget this formal-informal business. Several weeks into our new apartment a phone company representative called. The conversation went like this: "Hi, this is Robin from Midwestern Bell, are you Susan Tuttle?" "Yes," I replied. "Well, Susan," Robin continued, "it seems that..."

I didn't really hear the rest of what she said. My mind was whirring. She called me Susan. Did she know me? Had we met? Was this an old high school friend or something? So informal! What nerve! What ever happened to Ms. Tuttle? Or even Mrs.?

This happened at the doctor's, at the grocery store, at the pharmacy, the bank, the gas company, you name it. First name basis. The American equivalent to *Du*. And I realized I didn't like it. I wanted to choose to whom I get close to linguistically.

Back in Switzerland I adore the laughing chats with the owner of the drugstore, carried out in the formal *Sie*, although we could just as easily be *Du*. I was a little uncomfortable when at a social gathering I became *Du* with my doctor. I hope I won't need to see him for anything located lower than a sore throat in the near future. I enjoy the mutual pleasure of making *Dutzis* with new friends, and the respect I show elderly people with the revered *Sie*. There is a place for the different you's in this country, and I am happy finally to have found mine.

Happydog

"How old is he?" A voice from behind me inquires. I yank my panting giant puppy, Jake, back on his leash as he furtively tries to sniff the identity of the pooch who last peed against a nearby bush.

"Only six months." I feel a need to apologize because Jake is big for his age.

"Only? What breed is he?" Jake has now yanked me towards yet another bush. It is only then that I notice a tiny, furry thing at the end of a retractable leash sitting patiently at its owner's heel. I haven't yet been able to make eye contact with the human at the other end of the leash because of the 35 kilos of puppy-force pulling me in the opposite direction. But the furry thing I recognize as pure-bred and expensive. I only know this because I've seen the type on cans of dog food. They don't put pictures of mutts on cans of dog food.

"Uh, he's a mutt." Again, I feel like I'm apologizing because Jake's relatives weren't choosy. Jake has now noticed the small furry thing and gets down in his "let's play" position, tail wagging. Finally I can look my fellow dog owner in the face and I recognize that wonderful, heart melting oh-aren't-puppies-cute-look. I unhook his leash as Furry Thing's owner does the same. The dogs are on their own now, happily prancing and sniffing. The size difference doesn't daunt Furry Thing. He's got pedigree and age over Jake and knows it. Jake's just happy to have something which so much resembles a cat not running away for once.

I have officially entered the world of dog ownership in Switzerland and I've discovered it's a great way to get to know people. Suddenly strangers come up and talk to me in the street. Old women have actually walked up to me and praised me for taking the time to pick up Jake's droppings with the *Robidog* bag (little brown plastic bags conveniently available along favorite dog-walking paths). Even restaurant chefs have come to our table and offered Jake tempting tidbits from their kitchens as he peacefully sat under the table.

Owning a dog in Switzerland is a little like owning a Harley-Davidson motorcycle. It's pretty serious business. Most of the dog owners I've met have a big investment at the end of their leash. Even Jake, who is pure mutt on both sides, cost me something. I guess if I had got him for free, then he might not be considered a real dog. I got so tired of people asking me about his breed that I started saying he was a Chinese Fiesta Dog. Or an African Sled Dog. Very rare. Very expensive.

Sex is another fun topic. Complete strangers will shout at me from a distance of ten meters, "Is that a male dog?" I yank Jake back, who is amazingly precocious for his age and shout, "Yes, but he's too young still."

Looking relieved, the other dog owner will then unleash a female dog in heat. Jake instantly mounts her and I have a good natured, chummy chuckle with a stranger over my dog's inability to do 'it' properly yet. Jake mounts anything, but he's particularly fond of dogs his own size and human shins. It can get embarrassing. But a pooch's sex life is polite conversation among Swiss dog owners.

I don't want to mislead you about the wonderfulness of dog ownership. There are a few disadvantages. The *Robidog* bags, for example. I always have dozens of them with me. But when it really matters, like when he's done his business in front of the supermarket, then inevitably the only *Robidog* bag I have is full of holes and someone is staring at us. It's at moments like this that I thrust my hand into the shredded bag, hold it up to the light so every-one can see the holes, mutter, exclaim, check my pockets, and generally look exasperated. Then I tie the dog up near his mess so it is obvious I'm not abandoning my duty and go off in search of some suitable bit of trash with which to clean the droppings up.

And then there are the pedigree dog owners who have bestowed so many human qualities on their pets that the likes of a big, bouncy, ungroomed, smiling mutt like Jake are not welcome within sniff range. Like he could contaminate them, or remind them of what it's like to be a dog. My favorite story is that of the day Bo, a

lovely black Labrador, met a very exotic, long legged skinny white priss of a canine wearing a cloth coat. The owner was wearing a calf length mink. Bo bounded towards the pedigree in dog greeting style and the other dog, seeing the approaching non-human and none too pleased, tripped over its own feet and got a bloody lip as well as a tear in its coat. Telephone numbers, insurance company names, and anticipated vet and dog coat costs were subsequently discussed. So maybe a dog isn't always a way to make friends. But a lot depends on who you would like to be friends with.

Finally, there are dog haters. I think what they hate is dog messes on the bottom of their shoes. This is understandable. But they translate that hatred to include all canines and their owners. And they can be just as verbal as dog lovers. I walked by one the other day and he took the opportunity to tell the air around me that dog owners should have to pay 300% taxes because of the messes their dogs always left. I was carrying a loaded *Robidog* bag at the time and I can tell you, I had to battle the urge to waggle it in front of his face. Instead I patted Jake and thought that if a smiling giant Chinese Fiesta Dog can't win over a dog hater, I always had a loaded *Robidog* bag along . . . .

Baby blues

Nothing can really prepare you for motherhood. But I think I came into it with a few (American) ideas which had nothing to do with the ideas I encountered here.

The first shock came before giving birth. In my ninth month of pregnancy, the hospital sent me a letter asking for the baby's name. Naive as I was, I wanted to see the baby first. And the name had to be approved. I had a nightmarish image of some person at a desk sorting through names, tossing aside names he simply didn't like.

Then came the hospital stay – ten days! My dear aunt, mother of ten, claims they were the only holidays she ever had. To be fair I stayed five, feeling bored by day three, but not wanting to show up my roommates by recovering too quickly.

While there, I was instructed to put the disposable diaper on the baby backwards, tapes fastening behind – "to correct hip dysplasia." My inquiries as to whether or not Lucas actually had hip dysplasia went unanswered. That was the way to do it. I did it. Until I got home. Then I started taping in the front, at first a bit guiltily, then a bit more brazenly. Lucas promised not to tell.

When Lucas was 12 days old I packed him into one of those strap-on baby carriers and 'went public.' An old woman walked up to me and peered into the carrier. I obligingly lifted Lucas' hat a bit so that she could see him better.

With a clucking sound she shook her head and pronounced with all authority that I was crippling the child for life. I was shattered. What did I know? Displaced hips, crippled back – what else was I doing wrong?

Others kept volunteering advice. His hands were too cold or too warm and I shouldn't prop him up like that in the carriage. I should disinfect before nursing and weigh him before and after to be sure he got enough. Keep him out of drafts but nap him outside. And I was unable to catch on to the idea of putting underpants over the diaper (under the tights). Was the idea to train him (at eight weeks old) to wear underpants? It reminded me somehow of training bras.

The months passed and I adapted to my surroundings, my baby and the peculiarities of Swiss motherhood. Then, on a visit back to the States I horrified my female friends and relatives with my Swiss ways.

"Solids at three months?! Cow's milk at six months?!? He sleeps on a sheep skin?! And why is a boy wearing tights?" I was saying "hop-la" for "whoopsy-daisy" and "goo-goos" for "peek-a-boo". An American failure. One friend confidentially asked if they had pediatricians *over there*. I suppose it's the new mother's plight

to have lots of advice to add to the insecurities. But on two continents no less!

Fortunately Lucas' goos and gurgles helped bridge any gap he may have been experiencing. And that did it for me, too.

Scraps from childhood

I'm not one to get sentimental. I've learned through three overseas moves to limit attachments and be flexible. But as I drove through the Engadine Valley one day, I saw a scene which filled me with sentimental thoughts and made me mourn those attachments I coolly left behind. A little girl and her mother, both wearing aprons, were kneeling together in a well-tended garden bed beside an old house, sharing a smile. I could imagine the woman a child with her own mother thirty years earlier, perhaps in that very same garden.

I remember myself as a little girl playing house, the little mother with her dolls in the garden of my parents' home back in the States. And now in my Swiss garden I'm the real mother of two little boys. Much of what I expected of motherhood has become tangled in translation.

My sons Lucas and Simeon, armed with stories of Santa and Rudolph, can tell me about *Samichlaus* and his donkey. I memorized all the verses to *Jungi Schwän und Äntli* from a Swiss German songbook only to realize I had learned them in Basler dialect. The boys are learning Aargauer dialect around here. I imagined them having Sesame Street lunch boxes but got them Mickey

Znünitäschlis instead. Worst of all, I forgot to supply them
with costumes at *Fasnacht* – carnival time. I'd never have
forgotten Halloween. And I've had to put aside thoughts
of Little League, paper valentines, candy canes and school
buses. It seems as if all that came with me has to be put
away, scraps from my childhood left to scatter. I feel lost,
empty-handed.

I do make tomato soup, grilled cheese sandwiches
and chocolate chip cookies. My supplies of brown sugar
and peanut butter are as important to me as that well
stocked bomb shelter. But over at our neighbor's, are my
boys to blame if they don't eat all their *Rösti*? I confess I
get confused. Where to maintain my own tradition? Where
to start anew? Those mothers' intentions are meant well
too. Like them, I only want the best for my children. Yet
for as much as I want to see them integrate, I need to give
them what I brought with me.

I still murmur my love in English, and point out
black-eyed-Susans and snap-dragons. There are no noisy
bluejays or squirrels in our garden, but plenty of black-
birds and even a hedgehog. We'll plant our own pump-
kins to carve at Halloween, but we'll plant *Räbe* (tur-
nips) to carve too. And I'll never forget to prepare for
another *Fasnacht*. Maybe someone will drive by our garden one day and see me sharing a smile with my boys.
And maybe that person will become a little sentimental
too.

Tangled bridges

I am in a super-cool alternative community project playground. There is an entire boat, a big one, with an above decks and below decks. It is wood with lots of graffiti, an anchorless chain and a steel hull. It is sailing on leaves and mud. There are various wooden structures which look like dangerous fun. There are tangled rope bridges, a wheel-less car, even the nose end of an airplane, complete with cockpit. There are leaves in the cockpit. There is a long green slide with wriggles and bumps and curves, and an old wooden wash trough rocking in the mud. There are old tires nailed to wheeled boards, huge moldy saturated mattresses to fall onto, goal nets and hockey sticks.

This is a playground like no other I have been to in Switzerland yet. This place is more like a junkyard. A glorious, chaotic medley of unadorned stuff to climb on, hang from, push around and slide down. Stuff with lots of room left for imagination.

My kids go wild. They love this place. I pick up my son's jacket from a pile of muddy leaves and try to relax. The phrase "kids will be kids" runs through my head like a mantra as I try not to watch them dangle from rotting ropes and dart through an impromptu street hockey game.

Surely the soft ground will guard against painful injury. The hockey sticks carelessly clashing will magically miss tender skulls. Guardian angels must abound because this place is so right.

I am amazed to be here, in the middle of Berne, behind blocks of houses in an old workers' neighborhood. The park is a community project. Two male members of this community are present. One has dreadlocks, black high-tops and is walking up to a school kid who is busy sending a skateboard down the slide. He tells the kid to cut it out. The tone of the admonishment is universal. The kid smilingly agrees and dreadlocks walks back to the shed where he and a man with micro-short hair and a black leather jacket are busy chopping wood. I wonder whose fathers they are. Whose men. I'm attracted. I'm confused. I feel out of place.

Then two women enter the playground. They are around my age. They sport babies wrapped in exotic scarves against their chests. They stand upright and wear leggings with hand knit wool socks and combat boots. One sports a hennaed pony tail atop her head *à la* Pebbles Flintstone. The other wears a floppy green velvet hat and colorful woven backpack. They could belong with dreadlocks and black-leather.

I think I know something about them. They gave birth at home surrounded by friends and ex-lovers. They drink herb tea mixtures brewed in earthenware pots. They roll their own cigarettes. Their children have unusual

23

names and wear hand-sheared-dyed-spun-knitted sweaters in earth-tones or purple. Second-hand has political overtones not associated with financial necessity, as do bio-vegetables and whole-grains. They are strong and recognized by the men in their circle as being so.

I pull back my gaze and wonder if I stand out. I wonder why I feel threatened by these women. I look to my children to be sure that they aren't being noticed as belonging to an outsider. From this distance they seem as grubby and happy as the rest. *They are as happy as the rest.* Suddenly I know from where my discomfiture comes. It has nothing to do with our life styles and birthing choices, the clothes we wear or jobs we have. It has only to do with being comfortable with our choices.

I call out to my boys in English. This doesn't go unnoticed. I didn't intend it to. I tell them to be careful. They expect this of me. I feel better saying it. I exchange a curious smile with a super-cool-alternative-Swiss-mom. I am used to being the foreigner. And I realize she is too.

Stock up, Mary's coming

Wednesday morning, 9:20 a.m. I've sent my boys to school and have just found a parking place near my local grocery store. As on every Wednesday morning, I am doing a big shopping, enjoying the only hour in the week when both boys are in school at the same time. It was a bit more difficult to park this morning.

There seem to be more people around than usual. I'm too busy thinking of my shopping list to take much notice. But once inside, I discover that all the shopping carts are gone. Housewives are everywhere. I finally find a cart and begin to fill it, shoving my way through.

The bread counter is empty except for one package of pre-sliced English toast. The milk is nearly gone. A crowd of women is standing at the meat counter. I keep colliding with others whose grocery carts are stacked, for once, chock-full. I'm used to a bit of a crowd during the morning shopping, but this is weird.

I get in one of the checkout lines, wondering, is there some sort of sale that I missed? Or are all these people trying to be this store's one millionth customer? I find the answer on my way out: tomorrow, Thursday, the store will be closed all day because Mary is going to heaven *(Maria Himmelfahrt*, or Ascension Day*)*. Friday's hours will be the same as usual. While loading up my car I wonder if the boys will have school. Can I work in the garden? Can I hang the wash?

Switzerland's traditional and religious holidays always seem to catch me off guard; if Mary isn't going somewhere, she's being received. Thursdays can be green (Maundy Thursday) and Sundays can be white (Low Sunday). And then there is Happy Corpse Day (I always understood *Frohe Leichmann* – it's really *Fronleichnam,* the feast of Corpus Christi*)*.

In Zurich they have festivals like Sexy People Day *(Sächsilüüte* – which sounds to me like sexy *Leute* but really means the bells will toll six times to ring out winter*)*, not to mention the day when they shoot all the boys *(Knabenschiessen)*. Is that something like a turkey shoot?

One holiday I like a lot is in September: the day that everyone is supposed to stay in bed *(*actually it's *Bettag* – day of prayer*)*. Personally, I can't think of a better way to spend a Monday. And then you have the all-purpose religious holiday November 1, All Saint's Day *(Allerheiligen)*.

These days always come to me as a big surprise and if it weren't for the 'war's-breaking-out-tomorrow' attitude of the shoppers, I might even enjoy the bit of respite in the middle of the week. Except that the religious holidays always seem to fall on my wash day.

27

The 97-minute wash cycle

The last thing on my mind when I moved to Switzerland was the laundry. I assumed, in this modern land of technical wonders and cleanliness, that the washer/drier would be in the coin-operated laundromat in town where it belonged. It wasn't. And so began my education in the fine art of doing the laundry. Good-bye wash and dry, farewell Perma Press, hello wash kitchen.

I was introduced to the washing machine in my apartment block by the wife of the building superintendent. This formidable machine, securely bolted to a block of concrete on the floor, gave new meaning to the words major appliance. It could cook the clothes, wash them once or twice, spin them fast or slow and rinse them six times. And it took its time doing this. The longest cycle, double cook wash, took a record 97 minutes. The fastest took 45. I had been used to a choice of cold, warm or hot in 20 minutes or less.

Now I realize that not all the washing machines in Switzerland are like this, although the fact that they heat their own water instead of drawing from the boiler does mean they need more running time. I look longingly at the ads in the papers for computer-controlled multi-featured washing machines. I know friends who live in spanking new apartments with state of the art technology. But I also know that Swiss appliances are built to last, and the 30-year-old machine in the cellar of a 100-year-old apartment building is still chugging away to the rhythms of a housewife from the 1960s. Don't even think of replacing it.

I adjusted to this, but the absence of a clothes drier caused some serious withdrawal pains. The clothes never dried in the allotted hours they were permitted to hang in the damp, subterranean 'drying room'. That meant elaborate set-ups in the apartment. I warped the wood on the backs of three chairs before I finally bought a couple of those little folding drying racks. The plants always perked up in the steamy, damp environment wash-day created in my living room. And our faces became ruddy from drying them with stiff, scratchy towels.

Then there was the matter of wash kitchen schedules. Our machine had to serve the needs of 19 different households. One day every three and a half weeks I was allowed to get the key at 7 a.m. from the building superintendent's wife. Saturdays were not figured into the scheduling so that the residents could sign up for this day in emergencies. This emergency day was already filled in for the next eight months.

In my community the electricity supplying all the washing machines in town, private or public, is shut off over lunch to avoid an electrical surge as women turn on their electric stoves to cook a proper lunch. Obviously no one has bothered to tell the electric company that this is the dawn of the twenty-first century. That's why I must plan my wash-day with strategy and cunning. The loads are scheduled with an optimal usage of time. It's imperative to get the last morning load out and the first afternoon load in and running a few minutes before the shutdown to save an extra trip down when it turns back on. To save machine time I frequently stay with the wash and push the *Schnellgang* (overdrive) button when I think it's had enough. I can reduce the six rinses to an unhygienic two with this method. I keep a timer going in my apartment so that I can get down to the wash kitchen in time. Friends on the phone understand when I say, "Oops, gotta run. It's my wash-day".

Maybe this is a good sign. I can measure the degree of my integration by how well I manage the wash kitchen test. I could go on about wash kitchen etiquette, the long wash cycle controversy and how clean is clean, but I'll save that for another time. I have to put another load in. It's my wash-day.

Falling out of step

Tina and I used to visit the local fitness center together. We'd meet on Wednesday mornings for the step
aerobic hour. We were constantly in awe of the perfectly
coiffed and made-up women who would show up at 8:30
a.m., hand their adorably dressed and clean toddlers to
the babysitter, then slip into their two-toned Tonga leo-
tard and get into the aerobics studio early enough to get a
good spot in front near the mirror. I would usually manage to sneak into the back row after the music started,
wearing the sweatsuit which doubled as my PJs. Tina
would typically arrive a minute or so later only to vanish
several times in order to comfort her three-year-old who
wasn't keen on the babysitter. Neither of us had any in-
clination to wear make-up at that hour of the morning.
It's just as well the places near the mirror were all taken.

Giggling in the back of the room, losing the rhythm,
falling out of step, we'd later compare impressions about
the women we met at the gym on a weekday morning:
the moms and housewives, retirees, career women, ath-
letes. Were they here because, like us, they were trying to
revive a figure forgotten, defy gravity and time? Or because it feels good? Or because it's good for you? Or

because it's the popular thing to do? Fun didn't seem to be a motivating factor: the atmosphere was one of serious, sweaty business. But Tina and I found it hard to take ourselves too seriously considering nine out of ten times the two of us were stepping left while the rest of the class was stepping right. From the looks we received in the mirror, I'd say that here 'limber up' is not synonymous with 'loosen up'.

Once in a while an American aerobics instructor would show up at the center as a guest. It was a big deal complete with posters and a special sign-up sheet. I checked it out once. This guy's enthusiasm was overwhelming. There was this toothy, smiling, joking, energetic, let's-have-fun *Ami* shouting instructions, jokes and desperately trying to coax a flicker of enjoyment from the class that had been exercising very seriously for months without him. The grim looks on their faces reflected just how deeply embedded the work ethic is here. I swear I saw a full range of emotion cross over that grinning instructor's face as he tried to get the class to whoop and smile and dance along with him: hope, confusion, disbelief, discouragement, frustration.... He got neither a smile nor a sound, just determined, concentrated expressions. The class participants were busy getting their money's worth.

Tina moved to Southern California. And I had no one to giggle with at the gym anymore. But she came back for a visit and told me about fitness in America. I

was surprised to hear how seriously people take it there. Especially in her new neighborhood. The newest trend is to prefix anything you do with the word power. She told me about the intimidatingly beautiful sculpted bodies power-walking past her house at 6 a.m. before having their power breakfasts and going to their power jobs. Naturally they dropped their power children at the power day-care on their way. Suddenly the made-up Swiss moms and the determined faces didn't seem so foreign to me. At least I was able to be with them on a weekday morning. No way could I manage a 6 a.m. power walk before work.

Tina and I still sneak late into the back of the aerobic studios, but now they're 8000 kilometers and several time zones apart. She has promised not to prefix anything she does with the word power, and I have promised never to apply make-up before lunch. It's the only way we can be sure we're not taking ourselves too seriously. We're just doing our bit to keep things in balance. You know, going to the left when all the others are going to the right . . . falling out of step . . . giggling in the mirror.

Blinders and blinkers

It is Saturday morning and I have driven into the parking lot of our local supermarket. There is a gray Audi parked in the middle of the lot with its right blinker on. The driver is waiting for a woman who is lifting one item slowly after another out of her shopping cart and into a shopping bag in the trunk of her white Opel. She inspects each item carefully, checking for leaks, careful to arrange things in her bags. I can't pass the Audi, there's no room. Together, with the three cars behind me, we wait for the Opel driver to finish so the Audi can park and the rest of us can find a spot.

After a while the woman slams the trunk shut and looks up to see the line of cars. She squints at the Audi, wags her finger and shakes her head, indicating that she is not pulling out yet and walks away. The Audi doesn't even bother to turn his engine back on. Instead he switches on his left signal as another full cart passes us, heading towards a parked black BMW to the left. There are now six cars behind me.

Okay, I finally find a parking place. Now it's time to get a cart. The cart wants a one-franc coin. I stand there fingering my two fifty-*Rappen* coins. The change machine is out of order and the cashiers look stressed.

35

Here comes a lady in a navy wool skirt, sturdy shoes and a very sensible hair-do, returning a cart.

"Excuse me," I say, and lift my eyebrows and the corners of my mouth in what I think to be a polite, friendly look. I extend my two fifty-*Rappen*-coins and lift my eyebrows a smidgen higher. I hope this looks apologetic. "But may I take your cart? I don't have the proper change and the machine is . . ."

"Sorry," Sturdy Shoes interrupts while jamming the key from the next cart into hers. "I can't do that," she continues as her one-franc coin pops out. She holds the coin tightly in her fingers and finally brings her concentrated gaze up to meet mine. My eyebrows are now caught somewhere at my hairline and my face feels stiff. "You see, this is the coin I always have ready for the carts. If I give it to you I won't have it ready for the next time I need it, will I?" She pops it into her change purse and marches off. Holding my two fifty-*Rappen*-coins, I watch her disappear. I let down my eyebrows.

In the store the aisles are too small for two carts to pass. I am all too aware of the impatient shoppers behind me. So I try to be quick. I'll discover the rotten spot on the pre-packaged tomatoes and the expired 'sell by' date on the milk when I get home. There's no time to carefully shop with so many people breathing down my neck, trying to push their way through.

I collide carts with a young blonde. My eyebrows creep up my forehead again in a look of apology. They

seem to have a mind of their own. The blonde looks at a
point over my head and backs-up, avoiding my look. I
yank my eyebrows back down and mimic her own fur-
rowed brow and set my sights on the cat food shelves.

Finally I get in line at the check-out with a full cart.
A tiny old woman pushing a cart with a few items in it
comes up next to me. I try to catch her eye to tell her that
she could get in front of me if she wants. She looks dis-
tractedly beyond the check-out, like she's looking for
someone. At the same time she edges her cart in front of
mine as if I don't exist, just 10 centimeters away. Suddenly I feel aggressive. The muscles in my forehead and
cheeks are exhausted from trying to hold up friendly
looks. I let everything fall and nudge my cart forward
and effectively head off her attempts to squeeze in. Our
carts bump.

"Oh," I exclaim, not trying at all to hide my sar-
casm, "you don't have very much. Would you like to get
in front of me?"

She looks up at me, cloudy eyes magnified through
her glasses. She looks startled. I feel like a jerk. It dawns
on me that her pushing ahead isn't mean or malicious. It
isn't even done very consciously. And I don't think it
bothers my Swiss co-shoppers as much as it bothers me.

I smile at her, more genuinely this time, and let her
ahead. She thanks me.

While loading my car, I notice a red Ford with his
blinker on in hopes of getting my place. Should I keep

him in suspense and pretend I don't notice? That's not something I'd feel comfortable doing.

I turn to him and indicate that I'll be through in a moment and he can have my place. A look of relief spreads over the driver's face. And from the messages I get from my facial muscles, there is one on my face too.

Heidi on a Harley

It is difficult to write down the distinctive sound of a Harley motorcycle driving by. It is something like a *vroooommmm* mixed with the sound of loosely pursed, flapping lips. I recently followed this sound to a Swiss Harley-Davidson show. Harley owners and fans from far and wide converged for three days of alter ego wallowing. The bikes were clearly an excuse, beautiful and numerous as they were. The bikers themselves were the real attraction. A contest in attitude and looks.

Harley. American as apple pie. Visions of Hell's Angels, tough unemployed types with black leather jackets, tattoos, beer bellies, straggly beards and no smiles. Ditto for the women, minus the beards. Lots of sunglasses. Now turn that apple pie into *Apfelwähe*, add a substantial annual income, throw in a generous dose of Swiss perfectionism and cover the whole thing in expensive made-to-look-worn fringed leather and you've got the Swiss Harley owner.

It is difficult to tell the difference at first glance. But first you have to appreciate how much an imported Harley costs here. We're talking over 30 grand for a brand new factory model. That's *before* customizing. And no Harley owner in his right mind would drive a bike that wasn't customized. Hundreds of airbrushed paint jobs representing skulls, romantic Native American scenes, deserts, sexy women, flames, dreams, sissy bars, extended tail pipes, hand sewn leather seats, matching saddle bags, and, of course, chrome, chrome and more chrome. So we know right off the bat that these tough, scraggly looking types must have decent jobs. A Swiss Harley owner simply can't afford not to.

Now for the perfectionism. These guys probably chrome the inside of the gas tank. They painstakingly scrape the mud from the tire treads. They pay hundreds of francs for garage space to guard the bike from the 300 days of rain and clouds we get in Switzerland. They comb the continent for original parts. And they dream of a vacation with their bikes in Sturgis, Montana, for the really BIG Harley meet.

Am I making fun of the Swiss Harley fan? Yes, a little. Because the attraction isn't the bike anymore, it's the look that goes with it. Tough faces with a three-day stubble which will be clean shaven and friendly behind the teller window at the bank Monday morning, perhaps just a little hung-over in the transition. But I am also celebrating the alter-ego.

I discretely pointed out one particularly tough looking woman to my husband. Black Harley T-shirt with the sleeves rolled up to reveal flabby arms, cigarette dangling, tight jeans, micro short cropped hair on top with long straggly bits hanging down the neck, flaming red finger-

nail polish. Definitely no longer twenty but from the look on her face I would rather walk over hot coals than be the one to point that out to her. And suddenly I realized where I had seen her before. We had met a few years ago at a cosmetic party. You know, one of those female bonding rituals where we come together and discuss face creams with the Tupperware lady of mascara and lipstick. I also see her every Wednesday afternoon picking her kid up from drum lessons as I drop my kid off. Mom, housewife, neighbor.

The Harley babe. Yes, this role fit her much better. I decided not to go over and say hello. She looked so comfortable between the chrome and the tattoos and beer bellies. She was light years away from the cosmetic parties and drum lessons and kids I would remind her of. Monday would come soon enough.

Is that you, Santa Claus?

How does one start up a Christmas? It wasn't something I'd ever given any thought to before I had my own family.

In the years between 'leaving the nest' in the States and having my own family here in Switzerland, Christmas had become a quiet time at the end of the year which meant a break from work or studies, a chance to spend some time with family and maybe a chance to get away with my husband, Andy. My biggest obligations in those days were to show up on time for dinner invitations with nicely wrapped gifts, make a few batches of cookies for friends and family, and sleep late.

But once we'd had children, my dilemma began. With my family too far away to visit and the romantic days of lounging alone with Andy replaced by diapers, bottles, naps and kids' games, a feeling of dread arrived with the holiday season.

I expected Christmas to 'just happen' and felt frustrated when it didn't. I found myself with my own young family having to create the seasonal spirit myself. Sure we put up a tree and wrapped gifts, but suddenly it was all just work and I wanted to be the kid too. That's where my problem was; it was a matter of being grown up. I just wanted to go home to my parents and let them make the magic. I wasn't ready for this.

But ready or not, Christmas made its way into our home and our own version of the spirit evolved. I had a lot of help here in Switzerland. Christmas is preceded by a string of traditions which won't be ignored if your child is in the school system.

Simeon came barging in from kindergarten shouting "Mom, Mom! Adrian brought a *Mandarinli* for a snack today. Can you buy some too, huh? Please?" Seeing mandarin oranges in the stores is my first hint that Christmas is fast approaching. And it isn't even Halloween yet. So this week it's *Mandarinlis*. Next week it's peanuts in the shell. Then one of the boys cons me into buying a package of pine-cone shaped chocolates intended for the tree. They are consumed before we get to the parking lot. It's finally November.

While searching the attic for the wreath which goes on our front door, I hear *Guggemusig*, the cacophonous music which accompanies carnival time, being rehearsed at the neighbor's house. We must be up to November 11th. *Fasnacht* (carnival) should still be a few months away. But at the rate things are going, one can't be too sure.

Then one gray afternoon over tea, my friend Regi asked me what I do about the Samichlaus versus Santa Claus issue for the kids at Christmas. Kelsey, age six months, was perched on her mother's hip and sucking on the car keys, blissfully ignorant of the importance of what

I was about to say. Checking to see if my own boys were in ear shot, I narrowed my eyes and, with all the wisdom of years of dual-national motherhood behind me, I said, "Regi, if I could start all over again, I'd tell the kids right from the start that there is no Santa."

Regi's face fell. All her visions of creating and maintaining the Santa myth for her first born were suddenly clouded by my serious tone. "No, you don't really mean that, do you?" She pulled back, as if to shield Kelsey from my horrible revelation.

I really did mean it. I had tried too hard to make the Christmas spirit in my family and had gotten myself into a mess. I started off with the American Santa, someone I childishly hung on to. I thought he might automatically usher in all those Christmas feelings I so sadly missed. But then the kids started school and became aware of *Samichlaus*, the 6th of December and the *Christkindli* (a sort of Christmas angel). In all innocence, and with faith in the one true American Santa Claus, we let *Samichlaus* integrate into our tradition. He was the Swiss Santa, coming to check up on the kids before Christmas to see if they were worthy of a visit from the American Santa on Christmas Eve. The packages from over indulgent American grandparents proved it all.

The *Christkindli* was another matter. A Swiss friend told me how when she was a child, all the children would be sent out of the living room on the afternoon of Christmas Eve so that the *Christkindli*, notoriously shy, could magic in and set up a tree and presents. They were told that peeking through the keyhole during the magic would result in blindness: the *Christkindli* carried a long needle which he or she would not hesitate to poke through the keyhole. Of course, this was just one family's tradition. Still, it was enough to keep me from messing around with this angel. I had enough on my hands with two Santas.

Finding out about Santa should be a knowledge slow in coming, precariously coupled with that great feeling of being in on a grown-up secret and a little sadness. For my oldest son Lucas, it was a disaster. We had invited *Samichlaus* for his yearly visit on December 6, the Swiss Santa Day. Accompanied by *Schmutzlis* (Swiss elves, we said), he read about our boys from a holy-looking book. These things had been written by God himself, he assured us.

Lucas, just eight at the time, managed a slightly closer look at the book. When *Samichlaus* left, he dissolved into tears. "The words," he sobbed, "were written in ball point pen. God would use real gold ink."

It wasn't the false beard, the heavy make-up, or even the fact that we once saw Santa get into a car that spoiled it all for Lucas. It was the ink. Santa had lied.

I told Regi that I wish I had never gotten into this mess. Just then Lucas appeared. "Are you talking about Santa?" he asked. We exchanged conspiratorial looks. Then his little brother Simeon walked in. "How many sleeps 'til Santa comes Mom?" he asked. "Sixteen," I replied without even counting. Regi and Lucas looked at me. Simeon skipped out of the room singing. And Kelsey gurgled and chirped in her mother's arms.

Now on a fast slide into THE DAY, I belatedly light three of the four advent candles, dismayed that they are all the same height. However, all the windows on the Advent calendars have been opened. Our tree is waiting outside on the terrace and a CD of holiday music is playing with Louis Armstrong teasingly singing to Santa. I smugly think that this year I have found the perfect hiding place for the kids' presents. That Christmas will never be the same for me doesn't mean it can't be special. I take it to be a good sign that we've made the transition from being the enchanted to the enchanter. Now we can bring the joy. And isn't that what it's all about?

Fool on the hill

A Swiss friend brought me to a sports shop my first winter in Switzerland. "There's no way you can ski on those things you brought with you from the States," he said as a salesman smilingly appeared in front of us. "Those things" were a pair of used skis and boots of which I was very proud. They were a great bargain and I had only used them once on a hill in New Jersey. I had felt so proud, so *chic,* as I checked them in at the airport when I moved here. I remember when the lady at the check-in counter said "Zurich?" and I just smiled and nodded at the skis.

I learned two things at the sports shop that day: bargain skis are dirty words and the hills of New Jersey don't count. That was just the tip of the iceberg. I had been invited to go on a ski holiday.

I packed my jeans, long johns, down vest, wool sweater, knee warmers and knitted stocking cap. I even treated myself to a colorful wool scarf to be really trendy. I felt great on the drive to the mountains. Then, when we got out of the gondola at the ski area, I learned what trendy was. There were ski outfits that cost more than all the clothes I owned put together. There wasn't a single person in jeans. The only thing I had in common with anyone was the goose down inside my vest. I was grateful for the new skis and I concentrated on them all the way up the lift.

When we finally got to the top of the mountain, three T-bars and one chair-lift later, there were tears in my eyes. I didn't let on, but it wasn't really because of the cold wind. It was pure fear and dread as I stared down the slope. My stomach was in a knot. They didn't have hills like this in New Jersey.

I told my friend I wanted to take my time and enjoy the view. We agreed to meet for a coffee at the restaurant later. He pushed off and was gone. I positioned myself at the far corner of the slope. Every nerve in my body screamed "don't do it." As I slowly shuffled to the edge, gravity and the icy surface won out. I was moving horizontally across the slope. When I reached the other side I saw that I had gone down the hill about 2 meters. I calculated that with this zigzag method I'd be at the bottom by nightfall.

Two hours later we met at the restaurant half way down. "We must have just missed each other on the slopes. I got four runs in. Great snow, eh?" I nodded and ordered a coffee *Schnaps*. My jeans were soaked through and I had lost my new scarf. Melted snow was running down my back. My hair was damp and plastered to my forehead, my nose was dripping and my frozen toes were starting to throb as they thawed in my new boots. But the coffee tasted good, so I ordered another one and loos-

49

ened up a little as the *Schnaps* worked its way through my tensed muscles.

A beautiful girl at the next table had unzipped her hot pink and black ski suit to reveal a tight matching T-shirt. I struggled out of my wool sweater to reveal my thermal underwear shirt. She pushed her sunglasses up on her head and closed her eyes in the sunlight. I squinted in the glare.

A feeling of satisfaction came over me as my third coffee *Schnaps* was brought. "Hey," I said, "you know what that girl over there and I have in common?" My friend looked over at the sleeping beauty and looked back at me, perplexed and hesitant. I smiled. "We both skied down that mountain." He sighed a sigh of relief, and gave my hand a squeeze.

If you make it to Europe

It's amazing how popular we became once we moved to Switzerland. Friends and relatives with whom we had little contact back home suddenly were anxious to visit us. Feeling lonely and abandoned 'out here', we were equally starved to have them visit. I don't think I understood the impact a closing sentence like "... and if you make it to Europe please stop by!" would have in a letter to an old school friend who was stuck somewhere in Newark. Actually *knowing* someone who lived in Europe was as good as a ticket to go there.

And now it's that time of year again. Just as summer is starting to stretch out her lovely warm arms, someone drops a note out of the blue with a date, time, flight number and a cheerful "I'm on my way!"

I put away thoughts of a lazy holiday at home with a few adventures at the local *Schwimmbad*, think with a shiver of the inevitable trip up the *Jungfraujoch,* clear the ironing and bills out of the guest room and fill my ice trays.

What to do with visitors once they arrive has become something of a routine by us. The first thing which they usually want to do is open their suitcases in the living room and unload the 30-odd pounds of goodies I requested in response to: "...and is there anything you want me to bring that you can't get over there?"

Then there's usually an attempt at conversation which is soon abandoned to jet lag. I allow my guests a three hour nap, which they always claim they don't need while stumbling up the stairs. When I wake them later they always refer to the morning's events as having occurred yesterday. Of course, there are exceptions to this pattern, especially among visitors who are staying ten days or less. For example: my brother, upon arrival, unpacked a toy wagon in my living room, assembled it, pulled my kids to Baden in it, took pictures, shopped, stopped at a café, pulled home a load of chocolates, *Gipfelis* and beer, ate, drank, chatted and then, when I announced that I was ready to turn in, he asked if he could borrow my car to go explore the local night life.

Not all visitors are that gung-ho. One cousin who came to visit managed to stay on U.S. time for three weeks by sleeping on the couch until 2 p.m. every day. But most visitors want to get into the swing of things right away and want you to push. Last summer we had seven different sets of visitors pass through. We went up the Rigi six times, had *Rösti* and *Geschnätzlets* once a week, got to know the saleslady at *Heimatwerk* (a Swiss handicrafts shop) on a first name basis and could conduct a walking tour of Baden in 30 minutes. There is nothing like a helpless maiden auntie who comes for a visit to make you feel like Zurich is really *your* town as you astound her and yourself with how well you get around on the trams. Your faltering *Deutsch* is nearly always interpreted as fluent by your wide-eyed guests and it is shamefully easy to impress them with anything from a building from the 15th century to the size of your refrigerator.

I have a good time with my guests, but they tend to fall into two categories: Easy and Difficult. To qualify as an Easy Guest you played with my kids, wanted to do some things on your own, dried the dishes and didn't use up the hot water. The Difficult Guests hung around on the couch all day, never paid for their own coffee at a café, complained about what we didn't have and assumed that my kids would behave in all the shops and museums they wanted us to take them to.

But difficult or easy, I am grateful for my visitors because just when I start wondering "why am I still here?" they come along and show me a few things which I had stopped seeing, get me to appreciate where I am and help me to feel that this *is* my home. Not a bad feeling actually. And the bags of Cheez Doodles help too.

Coming of age

He's eleven years old. I was eleven the first time I visited Switzerland too. On my way out to the airport to pick up my nephew James, I feel myself nearly bubbling over with anticipation. The things I will show him! The mountains, the medieval villages. He'll be fascinated by the door handles and the cobblestones, the taste of the milk and the three languages on all the packages. A flood of memories from my first encounter with Switzerland accompanies me all the way to the arrivals building.

James doesn't seem a bit tired after the long flight from New York. We chat comfortably in the car and I nearly take his comment on the clean highway as a personal compliment. He's also impressed at the 120 km per hour we travel. I can hardly wait to show him around. Farms, trains, history, culture! I can almost see the place through his eyes. At least I think I can.

When we get to my house, my son Lucas grabs his favorite cousin and disappears with him and two skateboards. This is an important visitor for him too. I prepare a simple 'Swiss' lunch of *Bündnerfleisch, Fleischkäse,* and *Bauernbrot.* I want to introduce James to a drink that's a sweet memory of mine, *Himbeersirup* (raspberry syrup).

James catches on quickly. He makes the semblance of a bologna sandwich from the *Fleischkäse*, and politely drinks a glass of *Sirup*. Then he asks for a Pepsi. I only have Pepsi Light, which he drinks over a reminder that his mom doesn't like him to drink artificially sweetened drinks. For dessert the boys polish off a bag of Oreo Cookies James brought along.

The next day we pile into the car for a trip to Basel. The boys talk about rock stars in the back seat. Lucas is all ears as James describes the private lives of the members of the hard rock band Guns and Roses. A fan is born.

On the way to the Museum of Natural History we pass a CD shop. James begs to go in. I say we'll stop in later. The museum is a flop. The boys are too desperate to get to the CD shop to concentrate.

On the way back to the store, I can't interest them in the beautifully ornate fountains or ancient architecture. James goes right to the hard rock section. Lucas dutifully pads after him, all awe and wonder. Thirty minutes and 24 francs later we leave with a CD by the band Red Hot Chili Peppers. I've never heard of them. The words "generation gap" come to mind.

In the car on the way home James teaches Lucas the words to a song by Salt 'n' Peppa. Choruses of "Let's talk about sex, bay-bee" taunt me along the *Autobahn*.

At home again, James asks if we have any "near beer." I give him a bottle of alcohol-free brew. Lucas wants one, too. They listen to the new CD, drink the beers and dance in the living room. I go out and buy some regular Pepsi.

The time goes by quickly. We ski and swim, visit a cave and tour a few cities. James picks up some souvenirs along the way including a whip, a pair of toy handcuffs and a foam football with the words LOS ANGELES RAMS printed on it. A giant bar of Toblerone chocolate, his Walkman and a couple cans of Pepsi go into his carry-on luggage. He says good-bye to Lucas with a complicated 'high five' hand-slapping routine. I get a bear hug and realize how much I am going to miss him.

In the car on the way home from the airport I catch myself humming the Salt 'n' Peppa song. Lucas asks if we can get a CD by the Red Hot Chili Peppers too. He also wants a faster skateboard. I check my speed and drive on down the spotless highway.

Are we there yet?

"Are we there yet?" One half hour into our transatlantic flight and Simeon, our youngest, is raring to go. We're on our way to a four month adventure in America which will include relatives, Disney World, both coasts, a cross-country camping trip and a week at a beach house. A time for our Swiss-born boys to discover their American roots. A time for us to reconnect with our homeland. Are we there yet?

First stop, New Jersey. Predictably, Simeon steps off the plane with an ear infection. At the doctor's, he ignores her request to open his mouth. Aware that we have just arrived from Switzerland, the doctor draws her own conclusions and asks Lucas, the big brother, to ask him in German to open his mouth. Turning to Simi, Luke says, loudly and in English, "O P E N   Y O U R   M O U T H." He does. Are we there yet?

Next stop, Florida. We exit the airport into steamy heat. "I thought we were going to America!" Lucas cries. "But this *is* America," we explain. "Florida is a part of America." They don't get it and their confusion is legible on their faces. We got on a plane and flew to America. That's where Grandma and Grandpa live. Then we got on *another* plane and flew away. Are we there yet?

"Mommy! They're speaking Swiss German!" A couple and two school-aged children are walking ahead of us at Disney World. The father looks frazzled, the kids dazed and the mother resigned. Three days into a week-long Disney holiday, direct flight to Orlando, just like in the travel brochure. Jet lag and consumer overload look to be taking their toll. We get behind them in a line which promises a forty-five-minute wait for a two-minute ride. Are we there yet?

On to San Francisco. Down to work: buy a used van, register and insure it, outfit it for camping and head out. On the phone with the fifth insurance company to turn us down, I feel terribly foreign. Nothing like a little bureaucratic red tape to trip you up. No U.S. residence? No U.S. driver's license? No insurance. I finally locate a Japanese firm willing to insure our van. I have some trouble understanding the secretary's broken English. It's reassuring. Are we there yet?

On the road! We snake our way down the California coast, then head east. We travel through deserts and mountains and marvel at the star-filled nights. We resurface every few days for gas, ice and groceries, then plunge back into back roads, wilderness and campsites. I begin to feel that maybe we are almost there.

We've reached the half-way mark on our trip and we still have conversations which go like this:

"So, where'd you say you're from?"

"Switzerland."

"Wow, you hardly have any accent at all."

"Well, we're American. We just live there."

"Oh yeah? Nice over there, eh?" (Pats one of the boys on the head). "I'll bet these little blondies fit right in over there in Sweden."

"Switzerland."

"Oh, yeah. Right. Whatever."

I realized that my husband, Andy, had had his fill of these conversations when I overheard him tell someone in Nebraska that we're from California. Are we there yet?

The country has been crossed and we're ready for a week of 'real' vacation at a rented cottage on Cape Cod. We join the regulars who come here year after year for a week or two. We settle among them on the beach. Then one morning we commit the unspeakable: we come down to the beach a bit early and choose a cleared spot of sand about twenty feet north of the spot we've been occupying. A half hour later the last cottage group comes down. They set up a few feet north of us, casting glances. I realize that we must have taken their spot. The one which has been 'theirs' for the last ten summers. Andy rolls his eyes. I feel like a real outsider. Are we there yet?

We're on the plane, heading home to Switzerland. An elderly man sitting next to Simeon engages him in conversation. Simi is telling him all about our trip and how he went to America, Florida and the "Gram Candyon." He then tells the man we live in Sweden and that he can speak Spanish. I'm about to interrupt when Lucas tugs at my arm. "Mom, are we there yet?" he whines. I look past him out the window as the plane banks and we circle north-east, the New York skyline disappearing below us.

"Soon Lukie, soon."

Behind those closed curtains

When we moved into a semi-detached house in the suburbs I felt that I had finally moved into Swiss life. It was a real neighborhood – older, one-family houses with red tiled roofs, tidy gardens, swept walk-ways and PTT-approved mailboxes at each front gate. No traffic, no anonymous apartment blocks and, as it turned out, no other foreigners but us. No one really noticed us at first.

But something was askew. We weren't doing some things right. My trash would appear curbside earlier than that of my neighbors. My children would occasionally appear on the street still clad in PJs, or even less. I would arrive home with a week's worth of groceries in the car instead of the daily shopping caddy full. And I just couldn't keep up with the leaves which accumulated on our walk-way, let alone the weeds which overtook our garden.

I might never have given these things a second thought had I not felt myself observed, watched, checked. I realized that I had drawn attention to myself and that I was suspect because I was different. And suspicion is what guided the hand behind the white mesh curtain of my neighbor's window.

I would be unloading the car, yelling for kids to get in the house when my eye would detect that curtain move. I'd come out at 6:30 a.m. dressed in my night-gown to grab the paper from the mailbox and again, I'd see someone behind that curtain. Every visit to the car, the street or the mailbox, I'd find myself being observed. Early morning, midday or evening, someone was watching.

It started to get to me. I began to look for the shadowy figure behind that curtain. I became conscious of my actions and I felt myself getting annoyed. Then finally, the events of one Sunday morning motivated me into taking action. We were outside readying the bikes for a family bike ride. One child's bike seat still needed attaching, so my husband got out the drill in order to make one hole in the bike frame. The sound of the drill lasted twenty seconds. The seat was mounted, the tools put away and just as we were about to embark, a policeman walked up to my husband. "We had a report that someone was working." We explained what we had done, the policeman shrugged and said "that's not work" and he left. I looked to my neighbor's house and that curtain moved.

The next day I put my plan into action. I instructed my sons to wave whenever they spotted our neighbor behind the curtain. I did the same. I wouldn't let whoever it was continue to feel invisible. Our waves were always accompanied by our big smiles – welcoming, not malicious. The first few times the curtains moved

abruptly, the shadowy figure retreating. But eventually the figure remained. And then finally the curtain was cautiously pulled aside and there was a hesitant wave. Then one day a smile. A chance meeting, a greeting, a small chat. The children served as go-betweens, a kind of safe, neutral meeting place, an excuse to talk.

Since that time we have become neighbors. Herr and Frau Ernst are in their eighties. No children, very little family left and they are outliving all their friends. They built their house 50 years ago and moved in when they were newlyweds. They told me about the time that the lot on which our house stands was still a cornfield. About how difficult it was to get a house built during the war years. They built their house with a family in mind – unfinished rooms on the second storey were to be children's bedrooms. But the children just never arrived and the Ernsts lived on alone on one storey while the years passed and the neighborhood grew.

Their original neighbors who built next door, on the cornfield and down the street, grew old and moved out, or passed away. They watched new, young families move in, take over and suddenly, they were strangers. Then one day over coffee they confessed to me that they didn't feel at home anymore. They had become isolated and mistrustful, daring only to look at the world from behind closed curtains.

The Ernsts don't hide anymore. When I'm at the car or the mailbox they still observe me, but now they'll open the window and chat. We greet each other nearly every day. They give the kids chocolates. I shop for them. We look out for each other, smile a lot and share bits of our daily lives. Maybe they feel a little more at home now in their old neighborhood. I'm glad that they are there, watching, interested.

If they hadn't been looking out from behind those curtains I might never have gotten a chance to know them. And that would have been too bad for all of us because the feeling of home extends beyond walls. And the feeling of home is what I've been looking for.

Retail therapy

Shopping in Switzerland is a real paradox. You have a system based on honor and trust which defies crime. Walk out of an appliance store with a coffee machine worth over 1000 francs, and the store proprietor smilingly hands you a green payment slip because you forgot your cash. And he doesn't know you from Adam.

The local grocery store leaves unattended bins of produce or gardening equipment or lawn furniture out in front while it closes down over the lunch hour. At most, the items might be covered with a cloth to indicate they aren't for sale at the moment. Would-be thieves take the cloth to mean the items are not to be stolen at the moment. Now this is honorable.

It seems that strangers can be trusted to pay later. Crooks can be trusted to observe the lunch break. But what about customers who pay right away? Just try returning something to a store. Let me give you some examples . . .

Several years ago, after hours of looking and trying on, I bought a dress in an exclusive dress shop in Zurich. I got home with my purchase and realized it was all wrong for me. I instantly phoned the shop and said I was terribly sorry but I wanted to return the dress and get my money back. It still had all its tickets on it and my credit card receipt was just two hours old. No refunds, I was told. If I returned the dress the most she could do was give me credit to buy something else in the store which would be valid for six months. After that, the money, and the dress, was theirs forever.

I couldn't believe my ears. I talked to the manager. She told me the same thing. I told her I couldn't imagine needing anything from there again in the next six months. I told her I needed exactly that money to buy another dress someplace else. I told her a lot of things. "*Da chann i nüüt dafüür*," ("I can't do anything about it") was her cool and slightly irritated reply. Panicked, I phoned a lawyer friend. "Can the shop do this? Can they just keep my money and the dress?" I cried. "Yes, they can," was his reply.

I went back to the shop first thing next morning, frustrated and determined not to cry. I didn't want the dress, I just wanted my money, but I didn't think I had a chance. The manager was there, waiting for me. "Are you the woman with the dress?" she smilingly asked. I nodded, my carefully chosen and rehearsed German phrases mute in my brain. She lifted an eyebrow to the cashier who cheerfully relieved me of my package, produced my credit card receipt, tore it up and sincerely wished me a very nice day.

I recovered my bottom jaw from the freshly vacuumed carpet and slithered out. Had I gotten away with something? Was the exchange on the phone only intended to intimidate me lest I regret another purchase another time? She never actually said it, but I heard it all the same: "We'll let you slide this time, but don't let it happen again!"

It happened again. I brought two packs of Feta cheese back to the supermarket last week. Unopened and with a week to go before the expiration date, the cheese had fermented in the packages which had bloated alarmingly in the process. This had quietly taken place in the back of my refrigerator. The girl at customer service eyed me and the cheese and accusingly said, "You didn't keep this in the refrigerator. *Da chann i nüüt dafüür.*"

I defended myself. Of course I had kept it in the fridge. I buy this stuff all the time. What did she think, that I liked to buy cheese, wait for it to bloat then return it so I could get some new cheese and start all over? I wanted to eat the darn stuff, not do biology experiments with it. I held my ground and got new cheese. But I had to argue. I had to defend myself. I had to step down from the customer-is-king throne which I sat on with other American consumers. This must be cultural. Like haggling over prices in Middle Eastern countries. It had to be.

Of course, a lot depends on where you shop. Try the drugstore. Five salesgirls scurry up to me as I browse the shampoo aisle. After the fifth inquiry about my needing help in as many minutes, I start to get irritated. Aware of hurried whispering by the register, I realize it's The

Boss behind all this. An unattended customer must be the fault of an unobservant salesgirl. So I let the next girl help me. She's very helpful. I could tell her I need a shampoo for long, dry, oily hair with short, straight curls and she would find the product for me. Now I understand why there are apprenticeships in sales. This is serious business. I'm impressed and walk out with thirty francs worth of shampoo.

I've become a regular customer of that drugstore. The salesgirls leave me alone. It's The Boss who personally assists me now. He remembers my name, inquires about the family, and takes the time to discuss the pros and cons of various products. He told me about the socio-sex life of rats once, when I came in looking for some flea powder for my son's rodents. Sometimes he slips me a few extra Pro Bon stamps. Why, he doesn't even make me sign the release form for the poisonous drain cleaner anymore. He really makes me feel like a valued customer. Great tactic – it works. Here I really do feel like the customer is king. And you know what? *Da chann i nüüt dafüür.*

The real find
and other lessons

It was a little embarrassing, to say the least, having to explain to the insurance company how I rear-ended the car in front of me. It wasn't that I was unable to find the right words. No, it was the fact that I knew I was facing a cultural crevice that made it all so difficult. You see, I was driving along in a neighboring village and it happened to be the same day that this village was having a *Sperrgutabfuhr*, the day when you are permitted to deposit large pieces of junk curbside for collection. I rolled by many uninteresting heaps of mangled bikes and rusted washing machines, hardly even taking notice. But then suddenly I saw it. A lovely wicker chair, hardly frayed at all, just perfect for our terrace. A real find. At the same moment I neglected to notice that the car ahead of me had come to a complete stop.

I love *Sperrgutabfuhr*, especially in the wealthier communities. I'm a bargain hunter at heart and it's hard to hold back my enthusiasm about these perfectly good things destined for the dump. I guess I'm considered as a bit of an oddball around here because I've gotten some strange looks while pawing through piles of junk at the curb.

To avoid getting those looks, and to save a smidgen of my self-esteem, I've refined my junk heap searching. I have discovered that there are fewer observers over the lunch hour and at night. That's when I'll go for the larger items which I need the car to haul off. For smaller finds, I use my kids as cover. Under my instruction, they'll grab that old leather suitcase or wicker basket from the pile while I smile and exchange a look of bemused exasperation with the passers-by. We usually wind up with things like broken ski poles and two wheeled tricycles with this technique as well, since it's only fair they get to pick something out too.

Some people might think it's in bad taste to take what someone has thrown out. The rule is complicated though. Things which are cheap, used or free are taboo except in the case of close out sales (*Ausverkauf*), and, in some circles (mostly foreign), the thrift shops, second hand stores and Goodwill or Salvation Army stores (*Brockenhäuser*).

I'm quite willing to acknowledge these rules and risk looking a little foolish in my bargain hunting. But there is one area in which the attitude about used stuff goes too far: doggie bags.

Try asking for a doggie bag at a restaurant. Especially at one of those fabulous meals where they bring a whole platter of food and keep coming around to spoon a little more onto your plate. That leftover *Rösti* could be great re-heated with an egg for breakfast . But I just can't seem to make the waiter understand that I would like to bring the leftovers on my plate home rather than have him throw them out.

I tell him about my dog who just loves *Rösti* (or pork filet, or *Geschnätzlets*). He might finally agree to let me have the leftovers, but then he's at a loss as how to pack them. Needless to say, if I can get those leftovers home, the dog won't be the one to enjoy them!

But I've gone off on a tangent. I wanted to tell you about our car. The damage was fairly minor. A slightly crumpled hood and smashed grill for us, one broken taillight for the other guy. We glued the grill together and my husband straightened out our hood as best he could. By winter it had begun to rust in the creased places. Things would have been fine had our car not been called then for re-inspection. We brought it to the garage. The mechanic shook his head and asked why we hadn't repaired the hood properly in the first place. It would never pass inspection looking like that. We tried to explain how it didn't matter to us what the car looked like, so long as it still ran. He gave us an estimate which would have paid for a brand new five-piece wicker seating arrangement. We had to decide to either pay for the repair, or throw out the car.

There has to be a lesson in this someplace. I know there is. Still, I can't resist a good *Sperrgutabfuhr.*

Left holding the bag

Trash bag surcharge? No problem. I've learned to separate, condense and recycle my family's refuse. I dare anyone to find a scrap of paper, tin, aluminum, PET, glass or organic matter in my trash bag. Come down into my cellar and see the piles of bottles, cans, newspapers, scrap metal, old clothes, aluminum, batteries and returnable bottles I've got sorted. I'm used to this. Our garden is fertilized by our leftovers. I leave unnecessary packaging at the store. Yes, I've become good at this.

So it was with a smug chuckle that I read about the controversy over the trash bag surcharge when it was introduced in Zurich. Poor city folk, I thought as I carefully unfolded the flaps of an empty milk tetra pack. Finally they too will be forced to think about their garbage or pay their way with costly sacks. I inserted the flattened box into the last available spot of a bulging trash bag and tied it shut. It was the last bag of the roll.

"What?!" I exclaimed, incredulous, later that day. "There must be some mistake!" The checkout girl at the supermarket shook her head. No mistake. The surcharge on our community's trash bags had doubled on the first of the year. That meant a thirty-five-liter plastic garbage bag cost the equivalent of two and a half liters of gasoline! Careful me hadn't bought a new roll of bags in over three months. I took the expensive bags home.

I couldn't just forget it. I felt insulted. The nerve! After years of being a good, trash-conscious citizen, this is the thanks I get? I compost, collect, sort and recycle religiously. I allow half my cellar to turn into a recycling center. I bear the accusing looks of passers-by while inserting months worth of wine and beer bottles into the recycle bins (we had a few big parties, honest). After all this they go and DOUBLE THE PRICE??

I unroll one of the new expensive bags and shake it open. Then I yank open the refrigerator door. It is time, I have decided, to clean up.

Carefully I extract a recyclable glass pickle jar, still full of compostable bits of herbs and one lonely pickle. I tighten the lid. The jar makes a satisfying "plunk" as it drops into the sack. Then I toss in a half empty can of cat food, label, food and all. I'm grinning. Next: a shriveled carrot still in the plastic bag. A full yogurt cup, date expired, with an aluminum top! My satisfaction rises as I search the kitchen for more. The junk mail! Yesterday's newspaper! Coffee grounds! An empty beer bottle! Stale bread! An unflattened milk tetra pack! Breathless and heady with excitement, my eye falls on a scratched up Teflon frying pan. I dangle it over the yawning sack by its wiggly plastic handle. It makes a splendid clunk against the tins and jars. I tie the bag shut triumphantly. It's far from full. Another accomplishment: I've thrown away unused space!

My fridge cleaned, my rage exhausted, the glory of having spent Sfr. 3.10 my way rapidly dissipates. With a sigh I head down to the cellar to bundle newspapers for Saturday's collection. I'll bring the returnable bottles back in the morning, and maybe make a trip to the recycling depot, too.

Back to normal after my frenzy, I realize I have been left holding the bag. But I do feel a little better now, honest.

One of the girls

I rang the bell of my neighbor's house at the appointed time. The other six guests were already there, and the home salesperson, Frau Schmid, had set up samples of plastic products on the dining room table. As we gathered on the couch and chairs, I noticed that the other women had dressed up for the occasion. I felt a bit self conscious in my jeans and sweatshirt. There was no chatter, just an anticipatory silence as Frau Schmid looked over her guests and wares. My first Swiss '*Toopervare* party' (as the lady called it) was about to start.

In a shrill, no-nonsense tone, Frau Schmid reminded us that we already were familiar with *Toopervare* and she didn't need to go into all that. Heads bobbed in consent. She launched straight into her talk.

Holding up a mixing bowl, she assured us that it was not just any mixing bowl. This one had a lid with a hole in the top (re-sealable, of course) to enable the housewife to insert the electric mixer and not have the contents spray out during mixing. I have to admit, my interest was kindled as I glanced at the flecks of cake batter still adhered to my sweatshirt from that afternoon's baking. But wait a minute! This hole in the lid wasn't what was new.

That has been a standard *Toopervare* feature for a few years now. What really was new and special (and at this she flipped the bowl over with a practiced twist of the wrist) were the tiny rubber feet on the bowl's bottom! Breathless now, Frau Schmid explained how these little feet, combined with a unique design, virtually guaranteed that the bowl would not slide on the table during the mixing process.

She paused for emphasis. We sat there like a bunch of hypnotized chickens. This clever little feature, she went on, makes it possible for the housewife to mix with one hand, thereby freeing the other hand from the task of holding the bowl still. Why, the efficient housewife could probably manage to iron with the free hand while mixing with the other!

I tried to maintain a straight face as I visualized myself doing this. I wanted to burst out laughing. I glanced out of the corner of my eye to see how the others reacted. Dead seriousness prevailed.

The next item was a serving bowl which you could cook in. Visions of plastic melting over my stovetop flashed through my mind.

It turns out that you can pour boiling water into this specially insulated bowl, put in uncooked rice or noodles and after a while you would have cooked rice or noodles, piping hot and already in the serving bowl. But the real advantage of this little number was yet to be highlighted.

Appealing to the housewife and mother in all of us, Frau Schmid, with a well-placed sigh, told us how tough we have it at lunch time. One kid comes in at 11:00, the next at noon and hubby never walks in the door before 12:30, when kid number one needs to leave already. Now we're getting someplace, I thought. Frau Schmid understands!

In a conspiring tone, she talked to us, woman to woman, and got to the heart of the matter. How is it possible to have the noodles still hot by the time hubby walks in while junior is already done and on his way out? This special bowl, of course! There would be no more hanging out in the kitchen in those critical last minutes! And while no good wife is ever idle, we could use these handy minutes to finish changing the beds! Or sew on a button! The things we could accomplish then, the tasks that could be done!

I have to hand it to Frau Schmid. She really is a brilliant saleswoman. I realize that I'm afraid to take my housewife job seriously, in spite of the enormous task it is if done right. These women were professional homemakers. Suddenly I wanted desperately to be more like them. I needed to be accepted.

When she finished her talk, we got to fondle all the *Toopervare* on the dining room table, have coffee and cake and fill in our order forms. Dizzy with the amount of information I had received, I drank my coffee, ordered Sfr. 150 worth of plastic, ticked off the box "Yes! I want

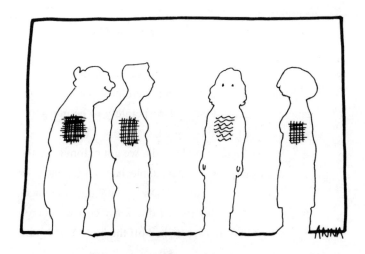

to be a *Toopervare* hostess too!" on the form and went home.

I was glad my husband was asleep when I got in. I needed time to formulate a way to convey the passion of the moment which swept me into my plastic buying frenzy. I crept into bed, wondering if he'd understand, or if he would even notice cake batter splatters on his freshly ironed shirts.

At the bottom of things

There are lots of ways to know a country, but getting sick in one can introduce you to a side of the culture you're not likely to experience otherwise. If you really want to know a people, suffer with them. You will experience an intimacy that gets down to basic subtle characteristics at the root of every national. It goes back to childhood and mothering. You might even say it lies at the bottom of things.

Now take your simple headache. Maybe you'll go to a doctor for it and he'll prescribe some medication. The same medication in Switzerland, France or Italy. A nice pain killer. Probably manufactured in Basel, but depending upon where you are, it may take a variety of forms.

Let's say you're in Italy. *Il medico* wants to give you a shot in the hip for that pain in your head. Your eyebrows knit. Your pulse rises and you begin to sweat in anticipation. He plunges in the syringe and you let out a howl. Suddenly you're Italian! Expressive, temperamental, lively. You hop down from the examining table, headache forgotten, full of fire (at least in the right hip) and limp out onto the street, feeling at one with the locals. Real medicine!

Well, maybe that headache got you in France instead. *Le docteur* prescribes some pills. You slink down to the pharmacy where the pharmacist discreetly wraps your box of pills in plain brown paper. Then you slither onto a chair at an outdoor café and order some water. Around you refined Parisians are chatting quietly over bottles of wine. You pop the tablets into your mouth and throw your head back with a flourish, rapidly guzzling sparkling water all the while. Conversation stops. Stares indicate a *faux pas.* You don't feel very French.

Finally you are in Switzerland. *Herr Doktor* sends you away with your headache and a prescription. The pharmacist hands over a package of suppositories. You look around to make sure no other customer has noticed. "Would you like a bag for those suppositories, Madame?" the pharmacist asks loudly. "Yes, yes!" you hoarsely whisper. Yearning for some French discreteness, or even a nice Italian shot, you scurry home and, well, follow the package directions. A concentrated and determined look on your face, you go back outside and blend into the crowd.

Cookies

The afternoon is gray and dull once again. The weekend seems eons away, at 4 p.m. it's too early to go to bed and I am struggling to keep out of my mid-winter gloom. Cookies! I'll bake cookies and fill the house with good smells, cheer up the children and make the time pass a bit quicker. But first I need to go to the store for the ingredients.

If it were December, I could buy kilo blocks of butter and boxes of 15 eggs on sale to take care of my Christmas baking. And all this would strategically be set up right at the entrance of the store. But now, right on schedule, the Swiss housewife has put away her cookie cutters and the stores have taken the emphasis off baking. Somehow, magically, aisles away from the flour and sugar, I find my cart suddenly full of paper, desk organizers, notebooks and plastic stackable drawers. How did this happen? I ask myself at the checkout. I came for butter! It's January, that's how. And true to form, the stores have decided that it is the time of year to clean up my desk.

The effect is amazing. Someone must have known that after the Christmas rush I would feel at loose ends and disorganized. January is notorious for its long gray days and distinct absence of holidays after all the New

Year's hubbub has calmed down. January is like one enormous Monday. And in addition, tax time is coming up. So some brilliant marketing man decided that stores should use the opportunity to push the stationary and office supplies. What better way to pull people out of that *Januarloch* (literally, the January hole) than by coaxing them with brightly colored plastic desk sets, blocks of clean white paper shrink-wrapped in handy stacks of five, ring binders in this year's fashion colors of purple and orange, alphabetized and numbered separators, and gleaming packages of sharpened No. 2 pencils!

How did that marketing man know I would be tempted to get out of my mental muddle by purchasing empty binders, blank paper and unused pencils? Fresh start! Clean slate! Repent, oh lazy ones! Get your lives in order and everything will be better!

It works. I staggered home with my purchases and lugged them up to the room which serves as my office. I piled them neatly in a cleared spot on my desk. I placed the pads of paper on top of the untouched pads I bought last January. Those pads were in pastel shades. These pads are white. And the pads I bought two years ago are of recycled grayish color paper. I'm about a third of the way through with those.

I unwrap the pencils and jam them into the new pencil holder. I write myself a note on a brand new bright green Post-it to buy some magazine files next time. I smile at my mess and think, yes, now I can clean up.

I lift some papers and start to sort through them. But within a few minutes I am overwhelmed. Something is missing. Glue? Tape? Notecards? Envelopes? I reach for the Post-its to jot a note. My euphoria is gone. The gloom starts to descend again. Then I remember what it is I forgot, what I need to get this whole thing going.

Cookies.

Snail casserole
with butterfly sauce

I used to complain bitterly about the Swiss school system because it sends kids home during free hours and for lunch every day, making it impossible for mothers to be anything more than turnstiles.

One kid home at 10, the other at 11, both out again at 1:15, and that's only for Monday. Tuesdays one kid wouldn't even leave home until 10, then they both were back at 12 to rush out again at 1:15. Try getting something done when every move was accompanied by yet another "Hi Mom, I'm home." And forget about working outside the home – this school system bases its hours on the adage: "A woman's place is in the home."

Okay, I was stuck at home, but I wasn't going to be stuck to stopping what I was doing every day to cook lunch, especially since it wasn't our main family meal together.

I arranged with a neighbor to have my kids go to her house for lunch every second Tuesday so I could have a day to myself. In return I took her kids the other Tuesday. It took a little convincing to get this going: "But I'm home anyway," she claimed when I suggested the lunch swap. I am mostly 'home anyway' too, but whether I'm at the computer or doing the laundry, I really appreciate the break from the lunch routine. She caught on too and eventually found things to do . . . like meet her husband for lunch, or start and even finish projects in one go. My Tuesdays were holy. I looked forward to them like a kid looks forward to Christmas. All mine.

Imagine my surprise when our community sent out a survey to see if anyone was interested in setting up a school lunch program. I thought this type of thing only happened in the bigger cities. I felt delivered from the Dark Ages. I could have wept for joy.

I was tempted to forge a few dozen names to the survey to make sure they saw that there actually was an interest (just in case I was alone in my desperation).

Turns out I wasn't alone. Within a few months we set up the *Mittagstisch Verein* – an organization which could supply kids with lunch and supervision for the 'free hours' between morning and afternoon classes three days a week. To the mothers sending the kids, it would give freedom to work, learn, clean, shop or even be sick or 'off duty' now and then. I could hardly wait.

I got on the club's steering committee. I went to meetings. I did fundraising, advertising, brainstorming. And finally, because no one else was willing, I volunteered to cook until we had enough funds to actually hire someone, which we estimated would be in about four months.

I felt very noble indeed, you know: loved the solidarity with working mothers, being community minded and all that. But to tell you the truth, I did all this only because I was eager for that shimmering oasis of three free days a week. This lunch program had to work because I needed it. I wanted it. No sacrifice was too big as long as the program got off the ground. And I had big plans for when I could hand my apron over to a hired cook. In the meantime, my days of cooking for a crowd of children became routine.

I steer my bike into the parking lot of the local church, unload the groceries, leave my bike unlocked, and let myself into the church's community rooms. I go into the kitchen and flip on the lights and turn on the dishwasher so it's ready to go later. I hang up my jacket, slip my apron over my head and start pulling out pots. Soon another mother, taking her turn as a volunteer, shows up. I'm happy when it's Marie-Therese. We work well together.

First grader Tobias runs in the kitchen. He loves to be first for everything, including the *Mittagstisch*. "What's for lunch?" he asks, eyes darting over the counters for clues. "Snail casserole with butterfly sauce," I reply and he rolls his eyes and giggles. It's what I say every day.

Three fourth-grade girls pile into the kitchen, cheeks flushed from the cold. Laura is already poking her head into pots.

"What's for dessert? When will you make those cookies again with the nuts? Can I have a carrot? Do you need some help cooking? Oooh, do you have new earrings?" They look hopefully around the kitchen and Marie-Therese engages them to help her set the tables in the dining room.

I try to cook 'Swiss' about once every week or so. You know, *Rösti, Geschnätzlets, Alpermagroni.* Subconsciously I think I do this to please the mothers. But most of the time it's American style. Sloppy Joes, meatloaf, casseroles, grilled cheese sandwiches, soup, pizza, lots of vegie sticks with dips. It's what I know best and the sheer novelty of it here keeps the kids interested.

After putting the food out on the tables, Stefano, a fifth grader, starts to act up. He claims he doesn't like what I've cooked, although he hasn't tried it yet and has never even heard of Sloppy Joes. He says he doesn't want to eat here anymore and flings a carrot stick at another kid. He has a lot of 'temperament'. Looks like he's had a bad morning.

I walk over to his table and put my hand on his shoulder. "Listen, Stefano," I say to him quietly in English, "if you don't settle down all the other kids will start up too and then we'll have a big problem on our hands. So just relax a while until after lunch when you can go out and play."

Stefano listens really hard, not understanding a word I'm saying. But he doesn't want the other kids to know that, especially after having put up such a fuss, so he nods.

He settles down. He eats his lunch. I'm relieved that this tactic worked – I have to watch it though, because it could backfire. Luckily today I have made Stefano's favorite cookies for dessert, so I know I'm safe.

At 1:10 the kitchen fills with kids coming by to say goodbye. I wipe my hands dry on my apron to shake hands – forever amazed at this mannered ritual learned in school. A few kids comment that they liked the food. Stefano shrugs when I asked him what he thought.

I get a hug goodbye from my boys with the comment from my son Simeon that Stefano doesn't understand English. It's useless to try to explain that that was the point – I think I've embarrassed him. Marie-Therese herds them out to get back to school and at 1:15 the place is suddenly quiet.

Now my volunteer days are over. The lunch program has gotten off the ground and I've taken a part time job. I really like my work, it pays pretty well and I get out of the house, which does wonders. A big bonus is that I can ride my bike to work and my hours fit in well with the crazy school schedule now that the kids can eat at the *Mittagstisch*.

Today, while riding my bike home from my job, I was aware that I feel enormously satisfied. The street was empty so I did wide, lazy turns down its middle. A stranger said "*Grüezi*" as I peddled by. This place is so familiar. I recognized Stefano walking on the sidewalk.

"Hi Susan! What's for lunch tomorrow?"

"Snail casserole!" I replied, slowing my bike.

"With butterfly sauce?"

"Yep," I nodded and rode on.

I'm the cook, you see. Happily employed cooking lunch so I don't have to cook. Makes sense, doesn't it?

Glue remover

When my oldest son Lucas was about four years old, he could, true to his age, be exasperatingly stubborn. If I needed him to get dressed NOW or come with me NOW or get his coat on NOW, he inevitably found a way not to do what I needed him to. He didn't understand time-tables or schedules or train times or clocks. He didn't understand that I needed him to cooperate so I could do things in the grown-up world.

At that critical moment when I was rushing around, nervously glancing at the clock and stuffing snacks and toys into a backpack before heading out to dash to the bus to get to the train, I would carelessly say, "Please help mommy and get your coat on, honey, we have to go now."

Lucas would sit stock still on the floor or bed or chair and announce, "I can't, my legs are glued."

When he would say this, he meant that he couldn't move because imaginary glue was adhering him to some fixed object. If Lucas' legs were glued, then there was no moving him. It wasn't a tantrum. There were no tears or shouts, no malice or mean little looks. Simply a statement of fact.

I came to think of it as a sort of natural phenomenon. He could make himself incredibly heavy, multiplying the laws of gravity by his age to the 68th power. And like most moms, I quickly went through the whole gamut of pleading, cajoling, threatening, ignoring, bribing and otherwise ineffectively motivating him to move. The few times I was stressed enough to pull the old 'I'm bigger and stronger than you' routine and physically pick him up, the spell would break – we would both end up tearful and angry.

So I tried the old 'beating him at his own game' strategy. I produced an invisible bottle of glue remover. I applied the remover elaborately and generously to his legs, with appropriate glooping sounds.

For the first few times this worked fine. But then he discovered he could prolong the game: once the leg was unglued, his foot became glued, then each unglued foot would become newly glued with each step. I tried to get him out the door (or into bed, the bath, or to the table) that way.

Then, after a few weeks of my going along with each twist he put into the game, he announced that the glue remover just didn't work anymore.

He had me there. So I left him glued to the bed one day while the rest of us ate dinner. He showed up at the table in time for dessert.

I got glued myself for a few years. But unfortunately no one was there with glue remover to help me out. When the glue wasn't working anymore, I found ways to make it work again. My glue was feeling sullen and foreign in a country that wasn't outwardly hospitable. My glue was my stubborn ineptness at learning a new language. My glue was feeling sorry for myself as an outsider, never facing the fact that I did make a choice. My glue was my crabbiness at a culture I didn't wholly understand, and didn't always want to.

Like the not entirely helpless little four year old, I rebelled by standing still. I raged at being misunderstood, I cursed the weather, the prices, the flavors, the schedules, I complained and commiserated with like-minded other foreigners, strengthening the glue that held me to my spot.

I added "not being able to write here" to the list. This was particularly painful because in the States, writing was important to me. It was a language thing, I claimed. I felt isolated and miserable.

Then I realized that everyone else was inside enjoying dinner.

It took me a few false starts to find a way out of my rut. After the 'feeling sorry for myself' phase, I entered the 'I'll be more Swiss' phase and promptly landed on my American butt. My *Rösti* was soggy, my housekeeping deplorable, and my accent a dead give-away. I couldn't be Swiss anymore than I could be Russian or French or Mexican. Then I entered the 'To heck with this, I'll be a foreigner' phase and I wound up feeling alienated from myself. Each attempt was like a new pot of invisible glue remover. I was drowning in the stuff.

Frustrated, I finally sought comfort in writing and the light went on. I wrote about my situation and experiences and suddenly I started to understand myself and the people around me better. And I started to feel better. I didn't need glue remover. I got myself unstuck.

As Lucas could tell you, life isn't that easy when your legs are glued. But writing about my encounters did help me gain perspective. Writing also opened doors to meeting people – writers, readers, foreigners, locals, newcomers, old hats. Writing and reading starts people talking and thinking and exchanging.

I'm at the dinner table. Things are happening there.

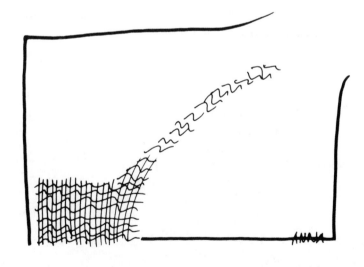

About the author

Susan Tuttle-Laube, originally from Teaneck, New Jersey, and now from Wettingen, Switzerland, isn't quite sure anymore where her American half starts and her Swiss half leaves off. But she claims it really doesn't matter because home is where her husband and two sons are, and where the laundry piles up. She's held a variety of jobs on two continents including: school bus driver, high school teacher, executive secretary, Chinese take-away counter girl, translator, factory worker, day-care provider, cook, advertising copywriter, editor, mother and homemaker. To make sense of it all, she always comes back to writing.

This is her first collection of essays in book form. Her stories have appeared in *Ticking Along Too* (Bergli Books Ltd., 1990 and 1996), *Cupids Wild Arrows* (Bergli Books, 1993), and various small press magazines in the U.S. and Switzerland.

About the artist

Anna Regula Hartmann-Allgöwer, better known simply as ANNA, is a passionate observer of people, inside and out. Art has been central to her since childhood, when she felt compelled to draw everything she saw. But after doing anatomical drawings in an art class as a teenager, she decided to study medicine, even though she always knew she'd go into drawing professionally. Her other passions include her family and friends and kitsch. She lives in Basel, surrounded by it all.

Her caricatures and drawings regularly appear in numerous Swiss and German publications including *Die Weltwoche, Tagesanzeiger, Nebelspalter, Frankfurter Allgemeine Zeitung, Sueddeutsche Zeitung*, and *Medical Tribune*. Her first book of caricatures, *Wechseljahre* (Zytglogge Verlag, 1996) has enjoyed enormous success and is in its third printing.

About Bergli Books

Bergli Books publishes, promotes and distributes books in English that focus on intercultural issues of interest to people living in Switzerland:

Ticking Along with the Swiss, edited by Dianne Dicks, entertaining and informative personal experiences of many 'foreigners' living in Switzerland from all walks of life and many different countries. They record their impressions, wonder, perplexity and assimilation. Includes essays, poems, anecdotes, letters and an A – Z on customs and foibles. ISBN 3-9520002-4-8.

Ticking Along Too, edited by Dianne Dicks, has more personal experiences of authors of different nationalities who live in Switzerland. Their stories are a mix of social commentary, warm admiration and observations of getting along with the Swiss as friends, neighbors and business partners. ISBN 3-9520002-1-3.

Ticking Along on Tape, an audio cassette of Swiss stories and sounds. Once you hear this selection of ten readings from *Ticking Along with the Swiss* and *Ticking Along Too*, you'll understand why these two books are so loved by 'foreigners' and Swiss people alike. There's playful irony, descriptive scenes, embarrassing incidents and touching experiences being told in a variety of Englishes with some very special and distinctive Swiss sounds. ISBN 3-905252-00-7.

Cupid's Wild Arrows*; intercultural romance and its consequences*, edited by Dianne Dicks, contains personal experiences of 55 authors of many different nationalities about living with two worlds in one partnership. These stories not only show the romance and excitement of such relationships but talk about the real-life challenges to be expected, the ups and downs, laughter, tears and peculiar situations. ISBN 3-9520002-2-1.

The Perpetual Tourist*; in Search of a Swiss Role*, by Paul N. Bilton, is an entertaining and light-hearted diary of an Englishman who lives and works in Zurich. Cultural values of the Swiss and the British have never been compared with such wit and insight. He reveals the pleasures and pitfalls of moving across cultural borders. This book is great for culture shock (getting it, not curing it). ISBN 3-9520002-3-X.

Soul Stripping*; autobiography of a go-go dancer*, by Paula Charles, is the touching story of this extraordinary woman who arrived in Switzerland with the wrong credentials, the wrong language, education, background and colour and found herself trapped in the seedy underworld working as a go-go dancer. She managed to stay true to herself in spite of the odds stacked against her. She takes you along on her journey to find a better life, love and approval and a way to stay out of the wrong corners. ISBN 3-9520002-5-6.

A Taste of Switzerland, by Sue Style, bears witness to the richness and diversity of Switzerland's gastronomic tradition and demonstrates the wealth of the local, regional and seasonal specialities which have evolved in Swiss kitchens over centuries. This beautifully illustrated book contains over 50 recipes to enable you to sample the food, folklore, history and traditions of this country of diverse cultures. The author takes you along on her visits to the country's best cheese-makers, vineyards, butchers, dairies, bakeries and chocolate factories. ISBN 3-9520002-7-2.

The Surprising Wines of Switzerland, *a practical guide to Switzerland's best kept secret*, by John C. Sloan, is an objective and comprehensive description of Swiss wines and of the work of the many interesting and dedicated wine-growers in all regions of the country. This book will be appreciated by wine lovers everywhere in their never-ending search for fine wines which are novel and uncommon. Includes a vintage chart, maps, addresses of selected wine-growers, a glossary, bibliography, index and 31 color photographs by wine-world photographer Hans-Peter Siffert. ISBN 3-9520002-6-4.

Berne; *a portrait of Switzerland's federal capital, of its people, culture and spirit,* by Peter Studer, Walter Däpp, Bernhard Giger and Peter Krebs. Berne is a city rich in contrasts: a modern capital with medieval landmarks, colorful, quaint, a little quirky – quietly international yet cozily local. Three prominent Bernese writers (a journalist, a film-maker and newspaper editor) share their personal perspectives, highlighting a wide range of subjects from history to the lively rock scene. Peter Studer's magnificent photographs portray the city's many moods, capturing the expected and the unexpected and Berne's easygoing charm. Discover why Berne is a whole way of life. This lovely book with over 200 color photographs will be treasured by residents and visitors to Berne. ISBN 3-9520002-9-9.

Dear Reader,

Your opinion can help us. We would like to know what you think of **Inside Outlandish**.

Where did you learn about this book?

Had you heard about Bergli Books before reading this book?

What did you enjoy about this book?

Any criticism?

Would you like to receive more information about the books we publish and distribute? If so, please give us your name and address:

Name:

Address:
City/Country

Cut out page, fold here, staple and mail to:

Bergli Books
Aeussere Baselstrasse 204
CH-4125 Riehen/BS
Switzerland